MINDFULNESS AND
PETS

PRISCILLA AN

childsworld.com

The Child's World®
childsworld.com

Published by The Child's World®
800-599-READ · www.childsworld.com

Photography Credits
Photographs ©: Dragon Images/iStockphoto, cover, 1,
7, 9, 10, 13; Ilona Shorokhova/Shutterstock Images, 3;
iStockphoto, 4–5; Shutterstock Images, 14–15, 16, 19, 20;
Ann Gaysorn/Shutterstock Images, 22

ISBN Information
9781503869677 (Reinforced Library Binding)
9781503880856 (Portable Document Format)
9781503882164 (Online Multi-user eBook)
9781503883475 (Electronic Publication)
9781645498605 (Paperback)

LCCN 2022951166

Printed in the United States of America

Priscilla An is a children's book editor and author. She lives in Minnesota with her rabbit and likes to practice mindfulness through yoga.

TABLE OF CONTENTS

WHAT IS MINDFULNESS?

Pets are an important part of many people's lives. They give people a sense of **responsibility**. Pets are fun to be around. They may make people feel relaxed. Pets can even help people practice mindfulness. Mindfulness is when people pay attention to their thoughts, feelings, and surroundings. This helps people stay **focused** when they are petting, feeding, or playing with their pets. Mindfulness can also help people create good habits when caring for their pets.

Goldfish need to be fed daily.

CHAPTER 2

FEEDING ALFIE

Ella hears a whining sound. She opens her eyes. Her dog, Alfie, is on the bed. He whines and paws at her. Ella groans. Today is Saturday, and Ella is not ready to get out of bed. She slowly stretches her arms and legs. "Good morning, Alfie," she yawns.

Ella sits up. She sees her ukulele on the nightstand. Maybe she can play a little before getting up. She plucks the strings. Alfie continues to whine. He licks her hand. "Stop it, Alfie!" she says.

Being a pet owner comes with a lot of responsibility.

Ella's mom comes to her bedroom. "Ella, did you just wake up?"

"Alfie woke me up, and now he won't leave me alone!" Ella says.

"That's because he needs breakfast!" Ella's mom exclaims. She picks Alfie up from the bed. "You know that's one of your morning chores. Why don't you get dressed before we go feed him together?"

Ella sighs and puts her ukulele down. She changes out of her pajamas and follows her mom into the kitchen.

Ella gets out Alfie's food. She pours some kibble into a bowl and places the bowl on the ground. "Here you go, Alfie," she says.

Many animals get into a habit of eating at a certain time.

TIME MANAGEMENT

There are lots of things to keep track of during the day. It can be hard to remember everything. Learning time management skills can help people be more mindful of their time. For example, people can make a checklist for each day. This can remind people to do important tasks such as walking or feeding their pets.

Giving pets the right amount of food is very important for their health.

"That is not enough," her mom says. "You need to fill the bowl, remember?" She puts Alfie down and fills the bowl all the way.

Ella huffs. "It's Saturday. I shouldn't even be out of bed yet! What if Alfie just wants a little bit?"

"Ella, Alfie depends on you to take care of him," her mom says sternly. "He needs to eat on a regular **schedule** like us, even on Saturday. Didn't you hear Alfie whine? He was showing you that he was hungry. If you are more mindful of Alfie, you can learn what his behaviors mean."

Ella puts her head down. She feels bad for Alfie. He was whining so loudly. He was probably *really* hungry! She sees him wagging his tail while he eats. She knows that is a sign he is happy.

Alfie finishes his food and drinks some water. Afterward, he jumps on the couch and barks. When Ella **approaches**, Alfie wags his tail. He lifts his paws and places them on her arm. What does Alfie want now?

Ella begins petting his head. Alfie lays down. He shows Ella his belly. But she continues petting his head. She likes to play with his soft, floppy ears.

Alfie barks at her. He bats her hand with his paw. Ella is frustrated. She thought he wanted to be petted! Ella wants to walk away. But instead, she takes a deep breath to calm down. She decides to pay closer attention to what Alfie is trying to tell her. She notices that he is still showing her his belly.

"Oh! Do you want belly rubs?" she asks. Alfie yips happily as Ella rubs his belly.

Ella is glad that she learned to be more mindful of Alfie's behavior. **Observing** her dog helped her know what Alfie wanted. Ella wants to be a good pet owner. She will pay closer attention to Alfie's needs in the future.

PETTING CLOUD

Jayden's brain feels like mush. He has just finished a full day of homeschooling. Today was especially hard. His math lesson had been challenging. Jayden sighs. But then he remembers it is time to play with his guinea pig, Cloud.

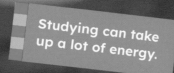
Studying can take up a lot of energy.

MINDLESS HABITS

After a hard day, it is easy for people to slip into mindless habits. These can include watching television or playing games for long periods of time. Mindless habits make people even more tired. Creating routines of mindful habits, such as setting a schedule for the day or focusing on mindful breathing, can help. Pets can also remind people to be more mindful.

Pets can offer comfort after a tiring day of school.

Jayden quickly changes from his school clothes to play clothes. He opens Cloud's cage. The guinea pig squeals when she sees Jayden. She runs to him. Jayden scoops her up and carries her to the couch.

As Cloud runs around the couch, Jayden closes his eyes. He leans his head back. His mind feels tired. Even though he does not want to, he keeps thinking about difficult math problems. He does not want to think about anything anymore.

Cloud sits on Jayden's lap. She nudges his arm. This means she wants Jayden to pet her.

Jayden laughs, shaking his head. He strokes Cloud's fur. It is warm and soft. When Cloud purrs, it feels like she is shaking against his hand. Jayden watches Cloud stretch. She sniffs the air on her hind legs. Jayden knows that she is probably looking for a snack.

Jayden gets a piece of cucumber from the refrigerator. Cloud whistles in excitement when Jayden brings the vegetable close. Jayden smiles as Cloud narrows her gaze on the snack.

Cloud munches the cucumber. As she eats, her eyes grow wider. Jayden listens to Cloud nibbling on the cucumber. Her crunching noises make Jayden feel relaxed. After Cloud finishes eating, she licks her mouth.

Cucumbers are healthy snacks for guinea pigs.

Guinea pigs can be great pets.

Being with Cloud helps Jayden pay attention to what he is doing in the moment. He is able to notice Cloud's feelings of excitement. When he pets her, he feels her warmth and her softness. Focusing on the present moment helps Jayden rest his mind. He is no longer thinking about his tiring day. He is able to feel more relaxed.

WONDER MORE

Wondering about New Information

How much did you know about mindfulness and pets before reading this book? What new information did you learn? Write down two new facts that this book taught you. Was the new information surprising? Why or why not?

Wondering How It Matters

What is one way mindfully interacting with pets relates to your life? How do you think this relates to other kids' lives?

Wondering Why

Even though pets cannot talk, they show their owners what they need. Why do you think observing pets can help someone practice mindfulness? How might doing this affect your life?

Ways to Keep Wondering

Learning about mindfulness and pets can be a complex topic. After reading this book, what questions do you have about it? What can you do to learn more about mindfulness?

THINK LIKE A DOG

Dogs have very strong senses of smell and hearing. Their ears perk up at the smallest sounds. They like to smell and explore their environments. Try using your senses like a dog would to be mindful of your surroundings.

1 With an adult, go to a park or other public place. Explore the park. Try to think like a dog would think.

2 Sniff the air. What do you smell?

3 Close your eyes and listen to the sounds around you. What sound sticks out to you?

4 If you can, follow the things you smell or hear. Where did you end up going? What did you end up seeing?

GLOSSARY

approaches (uh-PROHCH-ez) When someone approaches, she comes near someone or something. When Ella approaches Alfie, Alfie wags his tail.

focused (FOH-kusst) When someone is focused, he is paying special attention to something. Mindfulness can help people stay focused on their pets.

observing (uhb-ZUR-ving) Someone who is observing is watching something carefully. Ella learned where Alfie wanted to be petted by observing him.

responsibility (rih-spahn-sih-BIL-i-tee) Having responsibility means that a person has to take care of something. Pet owners have responsibility for their animals.

routines (roo-TEENZ) Routines are something that people do regularly. Setting a schedule of daily tasks or focusing on mindful breathing are routines that can help build mindful habits.

schedule (SKED-jool) A schedule is a set plan for events and tasks. Alfie eats his meals on a set schedule.

FIND OUT MORE

In the Library

Amoroso, Cynthia. *Responsibility.*
Parker, CO: The Child's World, 2023.

DiOrio, Rana. *What Does It Mean to Be Present?*
Naperville, IL: Little Pickle Press, 2017.

Hughes, Catherine D. *Little Kids First Big Book of Pets.*
Washington, DC: National Geographic Kids, 2019.

On the Web

Visit our website for links about mindfulness and pets:
childsworld.com/links

Note to Parents, Caregivers, Teachers, and Librarians: We routinely verify our Web links to make sure they are safe and active sites. So encourage your readers to check them out!

INDEX